Self-D

Producer

Develop a Powerful Work Ethic, Improve Your Focus, and Produce Better Results

By Martin Meadows

Download Another Book for Free

I want to thank you for buying my book and offer you another book (just as valuable as this one): *Grit: How to Keep Going When You Want to Give Up*, completely free.

Visit the link below to receive it:

http://www.profoundselfimprovement.com/sdp

In *Grit*, I'll tell you exactly how to stick to your goals, using proven methods from peak performers and science.

In addition to getting *Grit*, you'll also have an opportunity to get my new books for free, enter giveaways, and receive other valuable emails from me.

Again, here's the link to sign up:

http://www.profoundselfimprovement.com/sdp

Table of Contents

Prologue

The evolution of modern technology has led to the reduction in our ability to focus. Distractions rule our everyday lives. What used to be a normal ability—diligent, disciplined work—is now a superpower.

For many, not checking their social media profiles for the fiftieth time during the day is impossible. When browsing the Internet, most have dozens of tabs open, reading five articles at once, watching a video and responding to a message from a friend. Perhaps you are reading this book while eating lunch, or on hold for a call or avoiding the report you must finish today.

So many people constantly launch new projects that sidetrack them instead of focusing on one thing and doing it well. They constantly need new stimuli because having or doing the same thing is *boring* to them.

Self-discipline and good old work ethic are no longer attractive values. The need for variety and entertainment are what now dictate a person's behavior—at the expense of their productivity and ultimately, success in life.

Being unable to focus amid all the distraction makes consistency difficult. Building self-control, improving your productivity and delivering results day in and day out can be accomplished with a few minor adjustments. *Self-Disciplined Producer* will help you achieve success by teaching you how to make those changes.

As an author and entrepreneur, my income depends on my ability to focus. There's nobody standing by me, telling me to work. I have to implement strategic exercises and discipline myself or my business won't grow.

Distractions once ruled my life: instead of committing to a single business, I kept losing focus and moving from one shiny object to another. Needless to say, I wasn't capable of producing the results I was so desperately after.

Then a shift happened.

Over the last two and a half years, I released sixteen books, created four video courses with over 25,000 enrolled students in total, translated my books into ten languages, and created a YouTube channel with over 20,000 subscribers. As a result, I became a bestselling author in a wildly competitive personal development genre.

None of this would have been possible without consistent focus which I finally developed when I made a conscious decision to permanently improve my productivity. In this book, we will go step by step through the habits and strategies I discovered to help me deliver results, so you can see them in your own life.

I understand that you're a busy person with little time you can dedicate to reading. For this reason, this book—like my other titles—is brief and gets to the point as quickly as possible. Each chapter starts with the introduction of an enemy of focus and then offers you tips, exercises, and habits you can implement to overcome it.

Whenever I talk about work or being a *producer*, I talk about pursuing productive endeavors of all kind—working on your business, studying, learning a new skill, working for a charity, or performing any other value-producing task. Consequently, this book applies to all types of employment, professions and even your personal life.

By looking at five enemies of focus, including how they affect us and why we are susceptible, you can start making personal changes towards becoming a self-disciplined producer. This is why, throughout the book, for each challenge, there are multiple exercises or techniques that you can immediately implement in your own life to improve your productivity.

Eager to learn more? Let's discover the first enemy of focus at work and learn how to battle against it.

Chapter 1: This Common Habit Ruins It All

When a sudden burst of motivation hits Joe after watching an inspirational video before going to sleep, he makes a decision: the next day he will wake up at five in the morning and finally start building his dream business.

For once, the alarm clock doesn't bother Joe and he isn't tempted to hit snooze. After all, he's about to start the first day of his new, disciplined life. After a quick shower, with a cup of coffee on his desk, he gets to work. When searching for an idea for a domain name for his new business, he sees an ad about a new technology making thousands of people around the world rich. "I'll take a quick look," he decides and clicks on the ad.

Sixty minutes later, he realizes that he was supposed to buy a domain name. Instead, he has just wasted an hour jumping from one website to another.

With his attention back on the important task, he resumes work.

But wait, Kim has just texted him that she's free this evening. Everyone and everything can wait while Joe works on his business, but this doesn't apply to Kim. Thirty minutes later, having exchanged fifty or so messages with Kim, Joe feels hungry and heads to the kitchen to grab something to eat. He'll find a perfect domain name once his stomach stops growling.

Having satisfied his hunger, Joe is back to researching domain names. But look at this fascinating article—they say that an offline business can be more lucrative than a digital one. Yet again, Joe is sucked into an endless cycle of distractions: article by article, text by text, message by message, his control over his workday is slipping away.

Joe isn't an exception. A great number of people can't focus on one thing: they constantly need new stimuli and leave most tasks half-finished. If you don't believe me, then consider the following stats.

Only 45% of people spend more than 15 seconds on a page they visit, according to Chartbeat, a web analytics company providing insights to some of the biggest online publishers in the world like *The New York Times*, *National Geographic*, and *Harvard Business Review*. The numbers improve a little when they land specifically on an article page, with two thirds spending more than 15 seconds on the page[1].

According to video marketing company Wistia, 37% of viewers will finish watching an average 3-4 minute video, 42% will finish a 2-3 minute video, 48% a 1-2 minute video, and 60% a video shorter than one minute. In other words, most viewers are unable to maintain their focus for more than 1 minute[2].

2014 data from online eBook retailer Kobo shows that less than half of readers in the United Kingdom who purchased the top bestsellers of the year finished reading them. For example, only 46% of readers finished reading one of the biggest hits of the decade, a thriller novel *Gone Girl* by Gillian Flynn.

In North America, romance—the number one genre in terms of engagement—kept 62% of readers reading until the very end, while non-fiction managed to capture the attention of just 36% readers (seems like I chose the wrong genre).

Obviously, these statistics don't tell the entire story, but they do present a general trend: people lose attention rapidly.

In theory, there's nothing wrong with that. If a video is boring, why waste your time? If you notice an article or book that interests you more, why finish the one you're currently reading?

However, this common habit has far-reaching consequences that affect your ability to concentrate when working. Let's talk about several ways you can train your mind to maintain focus for longer than just a minute or two.

This or Nothing

When asked about self-discipline in the writing process, American novelist and screenwriter Raymond Chandler wrote the following words:

"The important thing is that there should be a space of time, say four hours a day at the least, when a professional writer doesn't do anything but write. He doesn't have to write, and if he doesn't feel like it, he shouldn't try. He can look out the window or stand on his head or writhe on the floor. But he is not to do any other positive thing, not read, write letters, glance at magazines, or write checks. Either write or nothing... I find it works. Two very simple rules, a: you don't have to write. b: you can't do anything else. The rest comes of itself."[3]

Note that this strategy doesn't *force* you to work—it's up to you whether you're going to just sit there, bored out of your mind, or do something productive.

When you limit your choice to boredom or productivity, the choice to get to work is easier. After all, for a modern human craving constant stimulation, virtually anything—including unpleasant work—is better than boredom.

If you can't concentrate, you don't have to work, but since anything even remotely entertaining is banned with this strategy, you'll probably manage to regain focus. Consequently, boredom can help you become more productive and creative.

If you suspect you won't be able to resist the temptation to cheat, a browser plugin to block the most distracting websites is a useful tool. If your smartphone distracts you, turn it off and put it in another room. If you don't need Internet access to work, turn off your router or go to a place without Internet access.

If your colleagues distract you, find a quieter place to work. If you can't leave your cubicle, put on noise-canceling headphones and warn other people that they shouldn't approach you while you work.

In today's world, few people ever do absolutely nothing. If you don't have a screen in front of you, then perhaps you're listening to music or a podcast. If you aren't listening to something, then maybe you're talking with somebody. Aside from sleep, most people never have many opportunities to get bored, think about random things and create random connections that often lead to breakthrough ideas.

Practicing the "this or nothing" approach will thus improve your creativity and develop your problem-solving abilities. I often get great ideas when walking, cycling, or simply sitting outside by myself, staring at nothing in particular.

Exercise: Eliminate Stimulation

Dedicate a portion of your working day to a single task and give yourself only two options: work on the task or be bored. No distractions are allowed. If you don't want to work, then don't work—but you can't do anything else other than just sit there and stare at the wall.

Start with a short period of time and gradually increase it as you become used to working without distraction.

When you refuse to occupy yourself with easy distractions in the form of social media, videos, articles, podcasts, distracting music, etc. you can finally dedicate all your thinking energy to the problem at hand and generate better results than you have ever seen before.

Perform Sets of Work

A powerful addition to the "this or nothing" strategy is performing sets of work. When writing, I usually set a timer to 25 minutes. After the allotted time, I give myself a few minutes of guilt-free distraction and then start another 25-minute block of work. This method is known as the Pomodoro Technique[4].

Your distracted brain can stay focused more effectively when it knows that soon it will be able to rest. Knowing that a break, even for just 5 minutes, is coming soon, makes it much easier to overcome procrastination and focus. The task at hand becomes less daunting than facing two hours of work with no rest.

If during the 25-minute period you find yourself craving a distraction, quickly note it down or bookmark the page you were thinking about and refocus on work.

When writing, sometimes a random idea or a topic unrelated to what I'm doing pops up in my head. I quickly open a notepad and jot it down, so I remember to check it during my break. The moment it's written down, the urge to distract myself goes away.

Remember, in just 25 minutes or less—which passes by extremely quickly when you concentrate on the task—you can indulge in distractions guilt-free.

If you find it too difficult to focus on a single thing for 25 minutes, start with 10 minutes or whatever is manageable and take it from there.

Working in sets is also effective for repetitive or overwhelming tasks. Prior to being an author, I was running numerous websites. I once set a goal to write 500 articles, each on average with 300-400 words.

It's a huge number of words to write (the equivalent of two full-length novels), and the fact that most articles were repetitive meant that the task was daunting and overwhelming.

I'm sure I never would have accomplished this goal if it weren't for breaking it down into sets of 12 articles a day, requiring on average up to six 25-minute blocks to write. In the end, it took me 42 workdays to get the task done—a short period of time considering how intimidating the task was.

Later, I used the same approach when I was learning how to write short stories. It took me a month to write a 400-page novel's worth of short stories, and again this number looks impossible to reach unless you break it down into chunks and work in 25-minute sets.

Exercise: Work in a Series of Sprints

Instead of trying to maintain perfect focus for a few hours in a row, work in a series of sprints. For example, work for 25 minutes, then give yourself a 5-minute break to do whatever strikes your fancy, and then resume work for another 25 minutes. A few sprints of work with heightened focus will be more productive than a few hours of distracted work.

Don't let the simplicity of this advice fool you. Try it for at least a week and I'm sure you'll see how powerful it can be. My writing career has flourished primarily thanks to this simple strategy.

Zero-Second Rule

Both aforementioned strategies sound good on paper, but often the struggle is to get started.

I know it from personal experience. On some days I start writing right away, and things go smoothly. However, sometimes I find myself switching from one distraction to another instead of getting to work.

That's when I use what I like to call a "zero-second rule"—the moment I realize I'm postponing work, I stop whatever I'm doing and immediately start working.

You have exactly *zero* seconds to ponder this topic any further—it's all about acting on impulse the moment you realize you're wasting time. The impulse helps you take the most difficult step—start—and then positive momentum will carry you forward.

Imagine that you're walking down the street and you see your role model—say, a successful entrepreneur or a famous singer—getting out of a car right in front of you.

If you give yourself time to think what to say or how to approach this person, you'll start coming up with excuses on why you shouldn't chat them up, even if it might be a once in a lifetime opportunity. The most likely result is that you'll walk past them, kicking yourself for your lack of confidence. If, instead, you act the moment you spot the opportunity and let momentum carry you forward, there won't be time to dilly-dally. You'll walk up to them and say the first thing that comes to your mind—and accomplish your goal of chatting them up.

The zero-second rule works in a similar way when it comes to productivity—the moment you catch yourself wasting time serves as a signal to immediately get to work. The longer you permit yourself to think about whether you want to work or how to get started, the more difficult it will be to start. Implementing a habit of getting to work immediately, when you realize you're wasting time, will train your default response to favor productivity over further laziness.

Obviously, it won't *always* work. You'll need to build a habit of acting immediately when you catch yourself slacking off, and you probably won't always act right away—just like you won't always be able to overcome shyness and chat up an interesting person. It will take a lot of training, but it will be worth it even if you fail on more than a couple of occasions.

Exercise: Get to It Right Now

Train yourself to get to the unpleasant task right away. You can do it in a variety of ways.

For example, when watching your favorite TV series while eating dinner, the moment you finish eating, hit pause and go take care of the dishes. It doesn't matter if you're putting them in a dishwasher or washing them by hand—what's important is to develop a habit of doing the unpleasant thing the moment it should be done, and not even half a second later.

If you make a mess in the kitchen while cooking, clean it right away before you decide that it can wait until you have more willpower to face it.

Engaging in the unpleasant thing immediately will help you build self-discipline that you'll need to overcome procrastination and get to work. The longer you wait, the more difficult it will be to start, so train yourself to get started right away.

If I have a particularly difficult day and can't discipline myself, I cheat my brain to get to work by writing just a few words, going back to whatever distraction I was occupying myself with, and then a short while later writing a few more words.

For some reason, switching the roles and using work as a quick break between distractions can often be enough to make you realize that getting to work is actually more interesting than the distractions. And as if by magic, you'll be also done with the problem of getting to work—you actually *started* working, even if just for six or seven seconds. Now you just need to continue, and that always proves to be immensely easier once you break past the first barrier.

Even if you don't always succeed with this strategy, your level of self-control will increase as a result of this practice and you'll find it easier to overcome the resistance to get to work.

Be a Finisher

A short attention span means that you probably have a tendency to leave things half-finished. Remember Joe from the beginning of this chapter? That's how a lot of people operate and then find themselves puzzled as to why they can't ever accomplish their important goals.

If you want to become a self-disciplined producer, you need to learn how to finish your projects. When you eat only a portion of your dinner, it will still provide you with some nutrition. Most tasks don't work this way—if you don't finish your project, you might as well have never started it because it isn't going to generate any results for you until it's complete.

There are three main strategies you can follow to become a finisher.

Strategy #1: Reward vs Punishment

In essence, finishing what you start comes down to one thing: the reward you get by completing the current task needs to be more attractive than the reward you get by switching your attention to a new task. Or alternatively, switching to a different task needs to come with a punishment that will make sticking to the current task more attractive.

For this strategy, you reward yourself with a cup of coffee or tea for each 4 sets of 25 minutes of work on the same task. If you fail to stick to the same task, there's no reward. Suddenly there are more consequences to switching to work on a new task— and that's precisely what will prevent you from leaving things half-finished.

Strategy #2: Switch, but Lose

Another strategy to help you become a finisher works in a similar way to the "this or nothing" strategy. You're allowed to switch your task, but you aren't allowed to go back to your previous task. Whatever you've already invested in your previous task is gone. It's this or nothing.

For example, if you tend to leave books half-read, start reading a new book if you want, but only after you get rid of the previous title.

If you're an author or a programmer, you can start writing a new book or designing a new app, but only if you permanently delete the previous draft or code.

If you're writing an email to a client, you can start writing another email, but first delete the draft of the previous message so you'll need to write it again later on.

If you're an online entrepreneur, feel free to start a new website, but first completely erase the old one.

How do you feel now about not finishing what you started knowing that it will go to waste?

Strategy #3: If Not This One, Then What?

Lastly, practice the "if not this one, then what?" strategy. I first learned about it through a blog post written by popular blogger Tynan[5]. Whenever you want to switch your attention to something else, ask yourself "If I can't stick to this task, what makes me think I'll stick to the new one?"

If you leave something half-finished so you can work on something else, can you trust yourself that you'll finish the new task, or will you leave it unfinished as well? What's the point of doing something else if you probably won't accomplish it, either? Ask yourself those questions whenever you feel tempted to switch—it might be enough to make you realize that switching doesn't make sense.

All of the strategies we discussed in this chapter focus on managing distractions in the short term. However, many of us have problems sticking to long term goals, which will affect your productivity even more.

Let's proceed to the next chapter in which we discuss why wanting things now means that most likely you won't get them ever.

THIS COMMON HABIT RUINS IT ALL: QUICK RECAP

1. A short attention span leads to consequences that affect your productivity. Engaging in behaviors like jumping from one website to another, leaving one article unfinished to begin reading a new one, or leaving books half-finished means that you can't maintain focus for more than a brief period of time.

2. "This or nothing" is a strategy that limits your options to just two: you work or do nothing. Given such a wide, attractive selection of options, most will prefer working.

3. In addition to "this or nothing," consider working in sets. The most common approach is the Pomodoro technique in which you work for 25 minutes, take a 5-minute break, and get back to work for another 25 minutes followed by another short break.

4. The zero-second rule is about developing an impulse reaction to procrastination. The moment you catch yourself thinking you don't want to do something is the moment you need to get to work.

5. There are three strategies that can help you become a finisher.

- **Reward vs Punishment** - losing your focus comes with immediate unpleasant consequences, and finishing your task brings a reward.

- **Switch but Lose** - you can start working on a new project, but you can't leave the previous one half-finished—you need to destroy it.

- **If Not This One, Then What?** - Ask yourself if you can trust yourself to accomplish a new task if you're giving up on the current one.

Chapter 2: If You Can't Wait, You Won't Get It

The second enemy of a self-disciplined producer is instant gratification. In a world where you can get anything you can afford almost instantly, it's difficult to sacrifice those instant rewards for a bigger, but not guaranteed future prize.

A cake in front of you is more tempting than a fit, strong physique a year from now. Buying this cool widget now feels better than saving money for the future. And in the same way, the instant entertainment you get from an amusing YouTube video, cat pictures, or reading news wins against the vision of hard work to build your business.

If you want to become more disciplined, you need to embrace *delayed gratification*. This means choosing to perform an activity that doesn't reward you much immediately, but over the long term leads to a big payout that instant gratification will never deliver. Work instead of slacking off. Exercise instead of watching TV. Vegetables instead of potato chips.

To embrace this attitude, you need to understand that anything worthwhile takes time. Computer architect Fred Brooks said: "The bearing of a child takes nine months, no matter how many women are assigned."[6] It's the same with most goals: no matter how much you'd love to achieve them as quickly as possible, it will take time and patience to get to the finish line.

Productive work leading to long-term results is neither glamorous nor rapid. It's putting in work every day despite hardships and discomfort, knowing that your compounded actions will eventually help you reach the results you're after.

But how do you embrace delayed gratification and maintain self-discipline if the process is so arduous? Different techniques work for different people so try a few and see what works.

5 Strategies to Embrace Delayed Gratification

The following are five of the most effective strategies you can employ to reorient yourself toward delayed gratification and increase your patience with the process.

1. Practice Long-Term Focus Through a Passion

As an amateur rock climber, my health—and sometimes life—depends on my ability to concentrate. If I let my mind wander while somewhere high above the ground, a mistake can be painful, if not disastrous.

My passions—even when completely unrelated to my work—have taught me how to become more self-disciplined, dedicated, and focused on the task at hand.

For example, when you're on a cliff, the world around you doesn't matter—it's you and the cliff. I now engage in the same level of concentration when writing—it's me and words on the page. Obviously, the negative consequences of losing focus when writing are non-existent when compared to the risks of climbing, but my work still benefits from the lessons I learn as a climber.

Krav maga, an Israeli self-defense system of which I'm a student, has taught me that even when things go wrong, you must keep going because nothing ever goes perfect, whether it's a street fight or life in general.

Delayed gratification is about maintaining focus on the end result. Essentially it's about sustaining a set of practices over the long term, for a positive, albeit delayed, outcome. If you want to have a fit body, you need to engage in the same healthy behaviors over and over again. If you want to learn how to dance, you need to perform the same moves until you can perform them in your sleep.

Having a passion is so powerful because while enjoying yourself, you develop traits and skills needed to embrace delayed gratification and achieve success in other areas of life.

Passions are so life-changing because they're never about a single *event*—they're about the never-ending *process* of improvement.

A passion—regardless if it's a passion for fitness, a certain skill like speaking a foreign language, or a hobby like woodworking—will help you experience on your own skin the power of long-term dedication. Then, based on *your own mistakes and triumphs*—not mere words written in a book—you'll understand that delayed gratification *simply works*, and that defaulting to idleness is a sure-fire path to never accomplishing your goals.

Exercise: Develop a Passion

Develop a passion for an activity that rewards long-term dedication. Before you know it, you'll find it dramatically easier to exhibit patience and stay productive even when the rewards are yet to come.

2. Learn From Others

What you read about successful people in the media rarely, if ever, portrays their true journey. It's easy to fall victim to the illusion that someone achieved overnight success, which then reinforces the incorrect belief that people reach success through luck or secret shortcuts.

Did some of the most successful people have it easier than you? Absolutely. Did some of them have it harder than you, but still managed to reach success? You bet. What is common among all of them, no matter their backgrounds, is that all of them had to delay gratification to achieve their goals. Nobody becomes successful without any sacrifices.

I strongly suggest reading autobiographies of people whose success you'd like to replicate to understand that they all had to put in work and delay rewards to build their dream lifestyles.

Peter Dinklage, world famous for his role portraying Tyrion Lannister in the widely acclaimed TV series, *Game of Thrones*, said the following in his interview for the New York Times: "I feel really lucky, although I hate that word—'lucky.' It cheapens a lot of hard work. Living in Brooklyn in an apartment without any heat and paying for dinner at the bodega with dimes—I don't think I felt myself lucky back then. Doing plays for 50 bucks and trying to be true to myself as an artist and turning down commercials where they wanted a leprechaun. Saying I was lucky negates the hard work I put in and spits on that guy who's freezing his ass off back in

Brooklyn. So I won't say I'm lucky. I'm fortunate enough to find or attract very talented people. For some reason I found them, and they found me.[7]"

It would be easy to say that he achieved overnight success. He appeared in *Game of Thrones*, the show went on to become a cultural phenomenon, and now Peter is a star. The reality—as explained in his own words—is different.

If you find it hard to relate yourself to world-famous Peter, consider my story. If you look at my catalog of books, you'll probably notice that my first book—*How to Build Self-Discipline: Resist Temptations and Reach Your Long-Term Goals*—is one of my most popular books.

On the surface, I'm an overnight success, right? My first book went on to become a bestseller. What you see, though, is the culmination of a long process that took well over a decade. I was writing short stories as a kid and have read hundreds of books. I wrote countless blog posts and articles for various websites and clients. There was nothing instant or overnight in my success—I worked for it for years, each day choosing to work over slacking off.

Exercise: Get to Know What Happens Behind the Scenes

No matter what the end goal of your work is—getting your boss to approve your project, graduating from college, building a successful business, becoming a musician, or developing a local non-profit organization—delaying gratification is the only way to go. If you're unsure of it, seek examples (like autobiographies of successful people) and learn what happened behind the scenes to understand that success never happens overnight.

3. Find Pleasure in the Journey

One of my favorite fitness experts is Al Kavadlo, a personal trainer specializing in bodyweight exercises. His feats of strength are impressive and his advice straightforward, but it's his philosophy of training that makes me enjoy his teachings so much. Search for his pictures online, and on pretty much every photo you'll see him smiling. Find a video of Al exercising, and he's always beaming, even when doing some of the hardest exercises.

Now compare it to a typical bodybuilder grimacing, swearing, yelling, and making every single rep look like torture. No wonder that most people who want to start exercising procrastinate. Why would they rush to experience so much suffering?

Exercise: Find Meaning or Enjoyment in the Difficult Tasks

If you suffer while doing something hard—or exercise, or anything in general—it *will* be difficult for you to stick to it over the long term.

If, instead, you focus on how incredible it is that you get to challenge yourself and grow (or find a different meaning of the task), the process will become easier to bear.

Whenever you catch yourself complaining about the difficult tasks, switch your attention toward the meaning or enjoyment you can draw out of them. There's always something positive you can find in even the most disagreeable tasks.

You need to understand that it's you who decides how pleasant the task you're performing is. In the end, only you control your emotional responses. It's your job to find pleasure in the journey—or to complain how grueling the process is and make everything harder for you.

Is washing dishes an unpleasant activity? Most would probably say so, but it's their *opinion*, not an undisputable fact. While I don't feel particularly passionate about washing dishes, I often feel good doing it because I like when there aren't any dirty dishes in my sink. I can't change the fact that I need to do the dishes, but I can change my way of thinking about this task.

Al smiles when performing hard, uncomfortable exercises. Something as simple as maintaining a smile when doing something unpleasant can help you deal with the unpleasant parts of the process.

Here are three additional ways to make it easier to work on difficult or frustrating tasks:

1. **Make It Less Complicated**. Create a repeatable system and use templates for the most common tasks, particularly the ones you don't enjoy. The clearer the process to follow is, the less resistance you'll feel.

I don't particularly enjoy writing book descriptions, so I created a template to follow. This makes the process of writing them less complicated, which makes the task less overwhelming and reduces the risk of me procrastinating on it.

2. **Express Gratitude**. If you're complaining how difficult or annoying the task you need to do is, realize that no matter how challenging it is, it's probably still better than the kind of hard, physical work most people had to perform daily a few hundred years ago (and some still have to perform to this day).

If you can't feel grateful for this fact, then at least appreciate that you have something to do that gives you some meaning.

3. **Think of Opportunities**. If you find it hard to feel excited about the activity, think of the opportunities that will open up once you get it done.

I don't enjoy the process of uploading my new book online, but I know that once I get it done, I'll be able to publish my book—and that makes the task appear more exciting and me less likely to put it off.

In addition to finding pleasure in delaying gratification, bear in mind that you aren't exactly losing all immediate rewards in exchange for future compensation. While working hard on your objective, you're getting several rewards today: the enjoyment out of doing something difficult, growing as a person, and improving your work ethic through consistent effort.

If you chose to be lazy, you'd get some instant rewards—arguably more pleasant than working in the short term—but nothing more substantial over the long term. In a sense, delayed gratification comes with more rewards: some instant (though perhaps less gratifying than the compensation you get from indulgence) and large future rewards (that you don't get when you choose laziness).

4. Control Your Desires

When you choose instant gratification—say, by putting off an important task—you essentially let your temporary desires dictate your future.

Obviously, none of us are superhumans capable of always choosing logic over emotions. If you're hungry, a craving for food may take you to a supermarket or a restaurant even if you're on a diet. If you're sleepy, you may fall asleep even if you have something important to do. If you're fuming with anger, you may say something you'd otherwise never say.

If it were so easy to control your desires, everybody would have perfect self-discipline and be as productive as they wish to be. While the reality is different, it doesn't mean we're powerless against our desires. With some practice, you can get better at self-control and learn to prioritize delayed gratification over instant rewards.

Think of it as training a muscle. A person who rarely fights against their desires has little ability to voluntarily choose something harder (put the work in now for a future reward) over something easy (getting a reward instantly). Conversely, a person who regularly engages in some form of self-control will consistently grow their ability to withstand the allure of cheap thrills and resulting lack of productivity.

As Stoic philosopher Epictetus once said, "Freedom is not procured by a full enjoyment of what is desired, but by controlling the desire."[8]

Here are some exercises you can perform to improve your ability to control temptations. Note that you should speak with your doctor before trying some of these exercises.

- **Taking Ice-Cold Showers.** Even if it's just thirty seconds, not defaulting to comfort by immediately turning on hot water is a good exercise in self-control.

- **Abstaining From Food**. Even if you skip just one meal every now and then, it will still serve as an exercise in developing more self-control.

- **Delay Purchases**. You don't have to immediately buy the new gadget, clothes, or try the new fancy restaurant. Wait at least a few days before deciding. Chances are you'll realize you don't need the purchase. In addition to training your self-control, you'll save money.

- **Delay Daily Pleasures**. If you usually watch new episodes of your favorite TV series the moment they come out, practice self-control by watching them a day or two later. If you want a piece of chocolate, wait fifteen minutes before you indulge. If you finished a hard workout, take a 10-minute walk or perform a brief stretching session before you head home to relax.

- **Work a Little Longer**. When you finish your work for the day, resist the temptation to switch into the play mode right away. Work for a few minutes longer to practice self-control and delay the reward—in this case, the moment you can relax.

Exercise: Push It a Little Further

Controlling your desires comes down to being able to tolerate some discomfort today for the increased benefits in the future. Exercise your ability to withstand discomfort by pushing your limits a little further when you find yourself exhausted, scared, or otherwise under pressure.

Exploring the borders of your physical or psychological limits can do wonders for your mental resilience and ability to stick to difficult things even when you presently aren't getting any compensation for doing so.

5. Practice Gratitude

According to scientific research, there's a correlation between expressing gratitude and increased patience[9]. A person who's thankful for what they have will be more likely to wait longer for a better reward.

It makes logical sense—after all, if you're happy with what you have, you won't desperately need another reward *right now*. You can wait for something even better *in the future*. On the other hand, a person dissatisfied with their progress, or in other words, feeling deprived, will be more likely to cease their efforts and choose to get an instant reward.

Exercise: Be Thankful

Regularly express gratitude for what you have and mentally pat yourself on the back for your progress. Acknowledging your small wins will fuel your resolve to keep going and keep waiting for the future rewards, while failing to feel thankful for them will negatively affect your ability to delay rewards.

Make sure to avoid expressing gratitude feel like a routine. Each time you do it, come up with new, *detailed* reasons why you feel grateful so that you can understand deep down that your efforts were meaningful —even if you weren't (yet) compensated in a big way.

Merely saying "I feel grateful that I completed this project" won't produce the encouragement and gratitude of creating a detailed mental picture like "I feel grateful for getting to engage in this new project that made me learn so much about client retention, strengthened my stellar reputation in the firm, and got me closer to getting promoted to a high-level manager."

IF YOU CAN'T WAIT, YOU WON'T GET IT: QUICK RECAP

1. Instant gratification is anti-productive. If you want to improve your work ethic, you need to embrace delayed gratification.

2. One of the best ways to understand the power of delayed gratification is to develop a passion for something that takes a long time to master, like a specific skill or sport.

3. Learn about delayed gratification through reading autobiographies and stories of people who put in consistent work without expecting any immediate rewards and were eventually rewarded for it.

4. When you find pleasure in the journey, it will be easier to delay rewards. To make the process more pleasant or easier, you can: use templates or repeatable systems; express gratitude for the task; think of benefits upon completion.

5. Practice self-control by controlling your desires: abstaining from food, taking ice-cold showers, or waiting a bit longer before you grant yourself a reward. The better you get at resisting

temptations, the more self-disciplined you will become.

6. Practice gratitude for all that you have in your life. Studies show that thankfulness makes people more patient, which in turn means you'll be more likely to postpone rewards.

Chapter 3: Does It Matter?

Few things matter as much as you think. Reducing your focus to the ones that do—and ignoring the ones that don't contribute much to the end result—is a key to increased productivity.

For example, I used to believe that to become a successful author, it was important to establish and grow my social media platforms. I thought that if I managed to attract over ten thousand Facebook followers it would visibly affect my bottom-line.

After spending time and money growing my platforms, I noticed that while my followers were engaging with my posts, they weren't engaged whenever I published an announcement about a new book.

I then realized that an author's popularity on social media has little to do with his or her book sales. Consequently, if your priority is to sell books, time spent growing your social media platforms is largely wasted. My experience has shown that few marketing strategies are more effective than simply publishing new books.

According to the 80/20 principle, discovered first by Italian polymath Vilfredo Pareto and further developed by American management consultant Joseph M. Juran, approximately 80% of the effects (for example business profits) comes from 20% of the causes (for example clients).

The proportion doesn't have to be exact and doesn't have to add up to 100%—it can be 90% of sales from 10% of clients or 100% of profits from 5% of products. The principle describes the phenomenon of the majority of the effects coming from the minority of causes—regardless if it's 80/20, 90/10, 70/30, 60/20 or 99/5.

In the original observation, Pareto discovered that 80% of Italy's land was owned by 20% of the wealthiest population.

Today, the data still applies in economics. In 2016, there were 186 countries on the World Bank's list of countries by their estimated gross domestic product based on purchasing power parity[10]. Just 22 of them—roughly 12%—are responsible for more than 80% of the gross world product. If we count the European Union members as a single country, just 13 countries—7% —produce more than 80% of the gross world product.

The 80/20 principle has been discovered to exist in a staggering variety of applications beyond economics.

As detailed in Richard Koch's book *The 80/20 Principle*, in business, 80% of the sales come from 20% of the clients[11] and 80% of the profits come from 20% of the products.

According to researcher Jakob Nielsen, in most online communities 90% of users never contribute, 9% of users contribute a little, and 1% of users account for almost all the content[12]. In this case, the relationship is 10% to 100%—10% of people create 100% of the content.

Other applications include fitness (a few compound exercises provide most of the benefits), health (most benefits come from just a few habits), work safety (a few hazards account for most of the injuries), and healthcare (a small number of patients use most of the resources).

The 80/20 principle is also present in personal productivity: only 20% of what you do contributes to 80% of your results. Or to put it in different words, most of what you do generates little to no results. Consequently, if you manage to identify and cut out the least result-producing tasks, you'll multiply your productivity.

For example, let's imagine that you work for eight hours during which you perform four tasks: A, B, C, and D. Task A is your most important task generating $100. Task B generates $50, task C $10 and task D merely $2. When you spend an equal number of hours on each task, you'll make $162 during eight hours.

If you cut task D and instead spend two hours more on task A, suddenly during the same eight hours you make $260 and become 60% more productive. Cut task C as well, and increase time spent on task A to six hours, and now you're making $350 in 8 hours.

This is more than two times the amount you earned before optimizing your workday.

Before you start your work for the day, scrutinize each item on your to-do list and ask yourself whether it belongs to the result-producing or largely ineffective tasks. If you can, skip it and take it off your to-do list. If for some reason you can't skip it (for example, your boss wants you to do it anyway), find a way to delegate it if possible. If you can't, batch all the low-value tasks and perform them *after* you take care of the most important job for the day.

It's easy to fall victim to the gratifying habit of crossing off numerous items on your to-do list, only to realize that the most important tasks are yet to be done. It's not the number of finished tasks that determines your productivity—it's your results.

That's why I'm ruthless when it comes to my own to-do list. It's rarely longer than a few items, and often there's only one item on the list—write 1000 words. I've identified it to be the highest-value activity for my business, so it's always on top of my list.

Exercise: Teleportation to a Desert Island

A useful exercise to identify the most important task is to imagine that you're only allowed to perform one task a day. Once it's done, you're teleported to a desert island where for the rest of the day all you can do is lie in a hammock and listen to the swaying palm trees.

How would your work day look if you wanted to feel satisfied with what you've accomplished prior to the teleportation?

Ups and Downs

80% of your best work comes from 20% of your efforts. This means that expecting perfect work performance all the time is unrealistic.

Obviously, the definition of perfect work is different for a surgeon and a programmer. The latter can afford creating code that doesn't work at first; the former can't botch a surgery and excuse himself saying that it's the 80/20 principle at work.

Please note that if 80% of your best work comes from 20% of your efforts, it doesn't necessarily mean that most of the time you'll produce shoddy results. It only means that your average performance will vary.

One day you might achieve more than you accomplished the entire past week, while the next day it might take you 4 hours to badly perform a task that usually doesn't take more than an hour. Sometimes you'll be satisfied with the result of your work, and sometimes you'll know that something is missing, but you won't be able to pinpoint what and how to fix it.

In rock climbing—and for that matter, any other sport—performance never stays the same. Sometimes I climb difficult routes I never expected to climb with much ease. A week later my performance is already bad during what should be a simple warmup.

On my down days, instead of despairing and worrying that my performance is lacking, I tell myself that it doesn't matter in the grand scheme of things. *This too will pass*, I tell myself. I do my best on both my best days and my worst days.

In the long term, it all averages out. Neither one day of incredible performance means that now you can expect perfect performance every single time, nor one day of exceptionally bad performance means that you're forever destined to fumble.

To give you an example from another realm, sometimes my writing is of high-quality and needs little editing after I finish the first draft. However, sometimes while editing my books I find myself being unable to decipher what I wanted to say and need to cut entire paragraphs.

I don't worry about it, though, because I know that 80% of the best content comes from 20% of my writing sessions. What's important is the long-term perspective in which both good and bad days average out. In the end, the only thing that matters is focusing on the big picture by putting in work daily and ignoring the temporary fluctuations.

Whenever you catch yourself discouraged because your performance isn't up to par, remind yourself that this too will pass. Do your best both during your good and bad days. It will all average out and result in a consistent performance.

Employ Occam's Razor

In the 14th century, an English philosopher William of Ockham developed a principle stating that among competing hypotheses that reach the same conclusion, the simpler one—with fewer assumptions—is more likely to be correct. The maxim is now known as Occam's Razor and is used primarily by scientists, though we can extend its application to productivity as well.

In its original form, William said that "Entities should not be multiplied unnecessarily," which in simpler words means that when considering a theory, we shouldn't multiply the number of moving parts beyond what's necessary. It sounds confusing, so let's go through a quick example before we move on to its practical application.

You come home and notice that your cat is nowhere to be found. The window in the living room is open. You can come up with at least two possible theories:

1. Your cat escaped through the window you forgot to close and is now enjoying the sunny weather in the backyard.

2. Somebody broke into your house, opened the window so that the cat could escape and disappeared without leaving any signs of his presence.

Both theories explain the same situation (your cat is gone) and how it happened (your cat escaped through the window). According to the Occam's Razor, the second theory is less likely to be correct because it's needlessly complex.

In the first theory, you have two agents—you and the cat—and two principal actions— you forgot to close the window and the cat escaped. In the second theory, you're adding a third agent—somebody who broke into your house and additional actions (entities) you need to explain—who it was, how he broke into your house, why he did so, why he didn't steal anything, etc. Coming back to the original maxim, you're multiplying entities when you already have an explanation that's equally plausible without them.

Okay, but what does all this crazy talk about escaping cats have to do with productivity?

Because a corollary to the Occam's Razor is the principle that if you have two equally likely solutions to a problem, you should choose the simplest. Or when applied to productivity, when you have two equally likely ways to accomplish something, go with the simpler choice. Don't unnecessarily add more entities if you can reach the same goal without employing them.

Successful real estate entrepreneur Gary Keller bases his entire book *The ONE Thing: The Surprisingly Simple Truth Behind Extraordinary Results* on the following question: "What's the ONE Thing you can do such that by doing it everything else will be easier or unnecessary?"[13]

Coming up with an answer to this question is a powerful application of the corollary to the Occam's Razor. Instead of needlessly multiplying entities by performing several tasks, find one task that can make other tasks unnecessary or at least easier. You'll simplify your work life and your productivity will soar.

In the case of my self-publishing business, writing is my one thing. I write and publish a lot, and on most days, it's my one and only task. Instead of engaging in dozens of little tasks, I rely primarily on my books to grow my business.

Many authors spread their attention over writing for their social media platforms and blogs, appearing on podcasts, pitching journalists, running countless paid marketing campaigns on advertising platforms, launching their books or other products on crowdfunding sites, and performing a multitude of other tasks.

Instead of simplicity, they choose complexity. In the end, they spend less time on their key task—writing—and more time on activities that could be to a large extent replaced by increased writing output (or a different strategy that would make other tasks unnecessary or easier).

It's not that the tasks they do are ineffective. Some authors succeeded primarily because of appearing on numerous podcasts, running successful Facebook ad campaigns, or because of a huge social media following. The problem is when an author engages in *too many* tasks and never chooses their primary one thing type of a task, condemning themselves to a complex and largely ineffective workday.

French writer Antoine de Saint Exupéry once wrote that "perfection is attained not when there is nothing more to add, but when there is nothing more to take away.[14]"

Instead of making your workday needlessly complicated, eliminate all but the most essential pieces. Try working one or two days without your complicated productivity system or a productivity app. If your productivity doesn't decrease, why complicate your life?

Obviously, not everybody can reduce their workday to one or two key tasks to perform. However, it isn't about doing just one or two tasks— it's about having the discipline to continuously eliminate the unessential ones whenever you can. High-achievers often feel the temptation to *add*, while in fact they should *subtract*—and then use the time they freed up to double down on what they do best.

Exercise: Seek Subtraction Instead of Addition

Develop a habit to constantly seek things you can eliminate from your work routine. The simpler your productivity system is, the better it will serve you.

> The less noise there is, the better you can hear the signal.

Embrace subtraction in other areas of your life, too. You might be surprised how many things masquerade as essential, but in fact complicate your life with little to no benefit.

Danny Kavadlo, one of the most successful personal trainers in NYC (and Al Kavadlo's brother who I mentioned in the previous chapter), notes in his video "My Name Is Danny Kavadlo. I Train Calisthenics" that you don't need the modern fitness equipment to achieve results. In fact, he believes that overcomplicated isn't always better—and his results based on performing exclusively bodyweight exercises prove it[15].

I used to train in my basement gym with free weights. When compared to people training at commercial gyms filled with complicated fitness machines, my workout was as minimalist as you could get. Yet, I still felt that for me personally, it was needlessly complicated.

I turned toward bodyweight training. Having discarded all the equipment except for a pull-up bar, I

60

could focus entirely on the movements in themselves. I no longer had to load weights onto the barbell, position my body properly on a bench, or worry that if I fail to perform a rep, the barbell would pin me underneath it. It was just me and the movement.

Even with nothing but a floor under my feet, I can still get a solid workout. I no longer need a gym. *Subtraction*, not addition helped me improve my fitness performance. What I had considered essential for years was in fact—at least in my case— disposable.

Another way to identify the unessential in your life is to limit the number of unimportant decisions by making your days repetitive. This way, you conserve decision-making energy to focus on what *does* matter.

I have fewer outfits than most people have shoes. Consequently, I waste zero time thinking what to wear, particularly since almost every article of clothing I own goes well with everything.

Similarly, I eat meals which would be considered bland by an average person. They might not earn any culinary awards, but I don't waste hours cooking sophisticated meals that ultimately wouldn't contribute much to my life (this might be different for you if you love gourmet food—it's a personal decision).

I follow the same work routine daily—with one priority non-negotiable task—so that I never have to waste time thinking what I need to do.

Exercise: Clean Your House

A quick exercise in embracing subtraction instead of addition is cleaning your house. How many items do you have that serve no purpose? If they don't add any value to your life, why keep them? Get rid of them and gain space—both in a physical and mental sense—for something that *does* add value to your life.

Treat your workday the same way. Question your long-held beliefs about what is necessary and what isn't. Clean the clutter and gain more clarity to focus on the essence.

As humans, we have a tendency to make things needlessly complex. Employ self-discipline to keep your life simple and reap the benefits. Increased productivity and a higher quality of life result from prioritizing and focusing on the things that will most positively affect your life. When in doubt, ask yourself: does it matter?

DOES IT MATTER? QUICK RECAP

1. The 80/20 principle is an observation that the majority of effects comes from the minority of causes. Adhering to this rule by identifying the crucial tasks and eliminating the low-value ones will improve your productivity.

2. It's impossible to perform perfect work all the time. Whenever you feel discouraged on a bad day, remember that ups and downs are a part of the bigger process.

3. The Occam's Razor states that a theory shouldn't be unnecessarily complicated if there already exists a simpler explanation. You can extend this principle to productivity by assuming that if you have two equally likely solutions to a problem, choosing the simplest one makes more sense.

4. Identify your one thing: a task that delivers such results that it renders other tasks unnecessary or easier to perform.

5. Develop a habit of questioning your long-held beliefs about what is necessary in your life. Make your days repetitive to limit the number of

unimportant decisions. A lot of what you do is probably provides little benefits. Getting rid of such things will help you maximize your focus on what *is* important and effective.

Chapter 4: Go to the Extreme

When I first became interested in self-publishing, I set a goal to write 3,000 words a day, which translates to about 8-10 pages. It was a challenging pace, but I wanted results as quickly as possible.

I was able to maintain this routine for a couple of months, but then one day found myself unable to progress any further. I pushed my limits too far and burned out.

The experience would have been a waste of time if it weren't for one realization: even though I couldn't keep the pace long-term, I learned how much I could accomplish when going to the extreme. I realized that exploring my limits, even though in this case I went well past them and suffered as a consequence, was a powerful strategy to boost my productivity.

Over the long term, staying balanced is a winning strategy. You can't expect to sprint the entire marathon or work 16 hours a day for years. However, if you never explore your limits, you won't know if you're pushing yourself adequately. Perhaps what you consider pushing yourself reasonably hard is in fact being a little lazy and you could increase your pace and still be able to maintain it in the long term.

Imagine a straight line. At the left side of the scale there's total laziness, and at the right there's ultimate productivity. Where would you place yourself on this line? How sure can you be where you are unless you push yourself to the limit?

Exploring your limits of productivity is like exploring your physical limits. You can't state with absolute conviction what the heaviest weight you can lift is until you actually try to lift it. And that's why you need to—at times—push yourself.

Move Past the First Limit

The first time you hit a brick wall when exploring the edges of your comfort zone, it's rarely your true limit. I like to think there are two kinds of limits: *mental* limits and *physical* limits.

For example, when rock climbing, you're pushing yourself to the limit only when you can't physically hold onto the rock anymore. You aren't done yet when your forearms are burning and you're afraid you'll fall. That's a mental limit you can push further. The physical limit is when your grip gives out and you can't do anything to stop it even if your life depended on it.

When working out, you're pushing yourself to the limit only when you can't complete another full rep with good technique. When you *think* you can't go on any longer, you hit your mental limit. You hit your physical limit when your body gives out and no amount of willpower will help you complete another rep.

When applied to productivity, unless you have a physically demanding job, physical limits aren't about your muscles giving out. Instead, they're about hitting mental exhaustion: the moment when you find yourself unable to concentrate any further.

However, you rarely hit mental exhaustion the first time you notice your attention slipping. Many people stop working when they *feel like* it's time to quit—but not necessarily when they're truly mentally spent.

Think of it as driving a car with a low fuel level warning light on. The fact that the indicator is on doesn't mean that you *immediately* need to go to the nearest gas station. Quitting the moment you feel the first signs of exhaustion is like thinking that a car with a low fuel warning light on is going to stop in the middle of the road immediately.

Exercise: Hit the Limit and Go Beyond It

To take your productivity to the next level, employ a rule that—at least periodically—you'll continue working despite wanting to stop. The second time you feel like it's time to stop, try to push yourself a little bit further if you can, even if for just a few minutes more. If you manage to continue, the third time you want to stop, finish your work for the day.

This little exercise will help you extend your true limits, and most importantly, realize that they largely exist in your head.

Early exhaustion is a completely *subjective* feeling. If you have two equally exhausted people, a

69

person accustomed to going past the first mental block might appear like they have more energy. The only difference lies in their mindsets. Both still have some fuel in the tank, but one person *believes* they hit the limit while another knows that the first limit isn't their true limit and so they can go beyond it.

Your accomplishments are largely defined by what you think is possible. Even if you fail while pushing your limits, you'll be still setting your sights high and moving toward your full potential. On the other hand, trying to avoid a possible bruising of your ego by not moving past your initial limits guarantees you'll never explore what you're capable of.

Please remember that pushing your limits doesn't mean being irresponsible. I'm not telling you to work for 24 hours without a break or perform handstand pushups when you can barely do five pushups. Pushing your limits is about exploring what you're capable of doing but doing it in a safe way. You won't be capable of doing much if you hurt or kill yourself.

Make It Intensive

One of the best techniques you can use to uncover how productive you can be is squeezing work into shorter deadlines.

In 1955 British author Cyril Northcote Parkinson published in *The Economist* a humorous essay in which he posited that work expands so as to fill the time available for its completion[16]. Today it's known as the Parkinson's law, and it's a fantastic strategy to help you get a task done faster than you think is possible.

In essence, the Parkinson's law is about exploring the extremes. If you think you need two hours to complete a given task, give yourself one hour. Did you manage to accomplish it in one hour? Then next time give yourself thirty minutes. You'll be surprised how often you can cut the time needed to perform a task in half, or even more.

How is it even possible that you can so dramatically increase your productivity by having *less* time to work? Because when given a shorter time margin to complete a task and subsequently, no luxury to dilly-dally, you'll probably work with more focus. If it's challenging to finish the task on time, you'll need to give it your best. There's no room for error, and you need to fully immerse yourself in an activity.

Obviously, it's not about doing the task as quickly as possible at the expense of quality. If you're responsible for servicing airplanes, you better take your time inspecting them. If you're a surgeon, don't set speed records. However, any other type of work in which the stakes aren't high is a good candidate to test this approach.

For example, I could tell myself that I'll write the next 1000 words within 30 minutes instead of the 60–90 it usually takes. Now, maybe I won't achieve it, but I'll definitely write with more focus and ultimately write more than if I were to give myself a more relaxing pace.

In writing, as in many other types of creative work, setting unrealistically short deadlines is also a powerful strategy to tune out the inner critic. With a short deadline, you can't afford to second-guess yourself. As a result, you unleash the full, unhinged power of your creativity. Perhaps the work will need some refinement later on, but the improved productivity thanks to the lack of self-censorship will be worth it.

Exercise: Set Unrealistic Deadlines

The next time you want to finish an important task more quickly, cut the time you usually give yourself to perform it in half. When you set unrealistic deadlines, you make the job more challenging, which leads to increased focus and boosted productivity.

It's important to note that I *don't* recommend using this strategy every day and for every task. While highly effective, it puts a lot of pressure to perform. It works like a charm when you use it sporadically but using it every day will make you reluctant to work.

Imagine you're learning how to box. Your coach wants to teach you the importance of holding your guard up, so he announces that during the entire workout he'll slap you hard in the face the moment you lower your arms.

The moment you receive the first slap and the world starts spinning around you, your focus goes into overdrive. You don't want to get slapped again—your cheek is still burning to remind you how stupid it was to forget about protecting your face—so you tune out everything around you and focus on holding your guard up. As you try to avoid further slaps, your focus dramatically heightens, and you acquire proper movement habits at an accelerated pace.

This strategy can be effective when used occasionally. If, you were to do it each workout, you'd probably grow tired of getting slapped. The best results will come from alternating between high-pressure workouts and workouts in which your coach reminds you verbally to hold your guard up so that you don't feel like fighting for your life during each workout.

Think about using the Parkinson's law in the same way. Use it to accelerate your progress, but not to such an extent that you'll discourage yourself from working.

GO TO THE EXTREME: QUICK RECAP

1. Temporarily going to the extreme can help you discover your true limits. Unless you push yourself hard, you won't ever know how productive you can be.

2. Your accomplishments are limited by what you think is possible. Moving past the first feeling of exhaustion will help you get closer to your full potential.

3. The Parkinson's law says that the more time you give yourself to complete a given task, the more time it will take you to finish it. Conversely, if you give yourself less time to accomplish something, it will most likely take you less time to reach it. Time pressure will force you to maximize your focus, and that will dramatically improve your productivity. Use this technique sporadically, though, as overusing it might lead to burnout.

Chapter 5: No Recharge, No Results

We've gone through some of the most effective techniques you can use to maximize your productivity. Now we need to talk about something people rarely think about when they are trying to get things done, yet it has a huge impact on your work performance.

I'm talking about *rest*.

Without recharging properly, even the world's brightest person wouldn't be able to provide genius insights. In the previous chapter, when I shared how I pushed myself to the extreme, challenging myself to write 3000 words per day, I burned out. Without a recharge, I was unable to continue that project in an effective way.

In a BBC article on the results of the world's largest survey on rest, professor Felicity Callard, director of the international group that devised the study, said: "We really need to challenge the assumption that if you take more rest, you are lazier. The fact that people who are more rested seem to have better well-being is an endorsement for the need for the rest."[17]

Millions of people suffer daily because they believe that working your fingers to the bone is the key to success. Obviously, work is indeed crucial. However, what matters is *smart and effective* work, not merely *hard* work. And working smart means that you not only focus on the work in itself, but also on proper rest. There's no point in working 16 hours a day, 7 days a week if 14 of those hours you can barely concentrate.

Consequently, in the last chapter of this book we need to talk about the proper techniques to recharge. This isn't merely about taking a break every now and then—it's about intelligent rest that not only renews your energy, but also helps you continuously achieve breakthroughs.

6 Top Methods to Recharge for Higher Productivity

As important as a proper work ethic is, if it isn't combined with proper *rest ethic*, you'll always operate at suboptimal level. Here are the most effective methods to recharge along with recommendations on how often to use them.

1. Spend Time in Nature

The cheapest and easiest way to recharge is to be spend time in nature. Studies show that taking a walk in a natural environment not only reduces anxiety[18] and rumination[19] (repetitive thought focused on negative aspects of the self). It also improves working memory[20] which, among others, is responsible for selectively attending to some stimuli (like the task at hand) and ignoring others (like noise outside or other distractions)[21].

Today, most of us live in stressful, noisy urban settings, but our primal nature hasn't changed. Big city living is a relatively recent change compared to the long history of living outdoors, not under artificial lights enclosed by four walls. We are still programmed to spend time in nature to feel at our best.

Develop a habit of spending at least one hour a week in nature. If you can, it would be best to leave the city altogether and go to a national park, forest, secluded beach, or a different type of a non-urban wilderness area. If it's not possible, go to a park, urban forest, or find a quiet spot at a city beach.

If you don't have easy access to natural surroundings, bring the natural environment to your home or workplace or at least surround yourself with some plants. According to a study designed by the scientists at the University of Exeter, plants in a workplace environment can increase well-being by 47%, creativity by 45% and productivity by 38%[22]. If you have some space for a mini garden—indoor or outdoor—establishing it can be a worthy alternative, too.

How often: as often as possible, ideally at least once or twice a week. Spending time in a natural setting is one of the most accessible and powerful tools you can use to manage stress and keep your performance at an optimal level.

2. Get Exhausted

Pretty much everyone already knows that physical activity is good for you, so I won't bother with citing scientific research about its well-known benefits. Instead, I want to point out one lesser known benefit that might encourage you to exercise more: improved cognition.

A systematic review of 14 studies on the relationship between physical activity and cognitive function has shown that engaging in regular exercise, particularly of aerobic nature, over a period of several months has been shown to improve the mental ability to choose what you pay attention to and what you ignore (known as attentional control), help process information more quickly, and boost the ability to suppress your urges and help you achieve a more important goal (known as inhibitory control)—like not eating a cake so you can lose weight[23].

Neuroscientists discovered that this happens because aerobic exercise causes the release of brain-derived neurotrophic factor, a protein that stimulates neurogenesis (the process of producing new neurons). Exercise also releases endorphins—feel-good hormones—that help regulate stress levels.

You can now see the connection: more neurons and less stress leads to more focus, better performance, and more self-discipline.

Engaging in light to moderate exercise will improve your cognition and make you more productive, but if your health allows you to do so, consider engaging in highly strenuous exercise as well.

It doesn't sound like it's a particularly recharging tactic to drive yourself to such exhaustion that you can barely stand on your legs, but there's a point to this madness. Strenuous exercise forces you to focus on the workout itself and few things can empty your mind better than a demanding workout.

As an adrenaline junkie, I prefer extreme sports. It's impossible to think about work when you're fearing for your life—even if you know rationally that there's nothing to worry about. I realize that not everybody is interested or can engage in such sports, though, so while I urge you to try them if you can, don't worry—regular exercise alone can also do wonders to your cognitive abilities.

At the same time, this serves as an example to find something that gets you going. Forcing yourself to attend a gym when you would rather be outside running or participating in a competitive sport will just be adding more work, and stress rather than rejuvenation. It is important to get exhausted in a way that excites you just as practicing extreme sports does for me.

How often: preferably two to three times a week. This is one of the most effective ways to reset your mind and at the same time, train your focus.

3. Work Lightly

There are two ways to recover from sports: you can have a passive rest day or an active one. During passive recovery you avoid all kinds of physical activity. The goal of active rest is to have a light, low-intensity workout to keep the momentum and aid in recovery. Some athletes also use active rest days to practice their technique without causing additional fatigue.

Apply this to your work for a balanced approach to productivity. Instead of staying away from work to recharge, you can try working lightly. It can mean working fewer hours, performing easy tasks, or working on something enjoyable only loosely related to your most important task. This way, you keep some momentum, but are still resting.

For example, while I generally try to write at least 1,000 words a day, sometimes I don't feel up to par. Usually I still push myself to get my daily word count in, but sometimes I choose active rest instead. During an active rest day, I might write only 200-300 words, work on the outline of another chapter, gather research, or perform other less important tasks.

How often: whenever you don't want to stop working but feel like you could use some rest. Note that it can't be your only style of rest. Full days off are still important.

4. Clean

Cleaning, as despised as it is by so many people throughout the world, can be a fantastic way to take your focus off work and get mental rest while doing something that needs to be accomplished.

Researchers at the Princeton University Neuroscience Institute found out that when your environment is cluttered, it hinders your ability to focus by limiting your brain's ability to process information.

It's as if the things you have around you were competing for your attention, taking up some of your brain's processing power and limiting your ability to focus[24].

For this reason, keeping your immediate surroundings neat should become a part of your work routine.

How often: as often as your place needs cleaning! On a more serious note, cleaning can mean something as simple as organizing your desk or even files on your computer. Taking two minutes to clean prior to beginning your workday can serve as a quick way to empty your mind.

5. Travel

Before I extol the benefits of traveling, there's no hiding the fact that travel is highly disruptive to one's routine. Each time I travel, I assume that I'll need at least the same period of time I spent on the trip to get back to my old routine. So, a one-week trip means I need at least a week to get back into my routine. It's a good rule of thumb you should be aware of, particularly when taking off a longer period of time.

However, as disruptive as traveling can be, you can't underestimate its powerful impact on recovery. Leonardo DaVinci once said that "Every now and then go away, have a little relaxation, for when you come back to your work your judgment will be surer. Go some distance away because then the work appears smaller and more of it can be taken in at a glance and a lack of harmony and proportion is more readily seen."

By putting both physical and mental distance between you and your work, you'll have an easier time resetting your mind. Instead of thinking through the same problems over and over, you focus on exploring the new surroundings and experiencing new things. Then, when you come back, you'll look at the world—and your problems—from a fresh perspective.

How often: at least once a year, and preferably once a quarter. Note that you don't have to take weeks off—a few weekend trips plus at least one weeklong trip a year will do.

6. Meditate

The mere act of sitting comfortably with your mind focused on the breath can do wonders to help you feel calmer, and consequently better able to manage your thoughts and improve your work performance. Countless studies have proven numerous benefits of meditation, with stress reduction being the most important one for people seeking to improve their productivity[25].

If traditional meditation is not your thing, engage in a different type of a meditative practice. Examples include: engaging in a high-focus sport (like boxing), playing musical instruments, or practicing skills that require precision (like knitting or woodworking). Anything that makes you mindful and focused on the present moment is a solid alternative.

The specifics of meditation are beyond the scope of this book. I strongly suggest reading Chade-Meng Tan's books *Search Inside Yourself* and *Joy on Demand*, both of which provide easy to follow instructions on how to introduce the meditation habit in your life.

How often: ideally every day for at least 5-10 minutes, though if you're strapped for time, even one minute of mindful breathing can have a positive impact on your performance.

NO RECHARGE, NO RESULTS: QUICK RECAP

1. You can't be productive all the time without proper rest. Resist the temptation to think that more is better—working 16-hour days serves no purpose if 14 of those hours you can't focus.

2. Spending time in nature has been proven to be one of the best ways to recharge. It not only reduces stress, but also improves working memory and focus. Surround yourself with nature as often as possible.

3. Physical activity improves your cognition in a variety of ways, including improving your attentional control, inhibitory control and information processing speed. If you can, engage in strenuous exercise as it's a perfect way to empty your mind. Do it at least twice a week.

4. Working lightly is a form of active rest. Instead of taking an entire day off, perform some easy tasks or work for just a short period of time. This way, you can keep the positive momentum going until you're ready to take an entire day off.

5. Decluttering your surroundings will free up some of your brainpower to focus on the important tasks. Periodically clean your immediate work environment to ensure maximum productivity. Remove unnecessary items.

6. Traveling will help you look at the world from a fresh perspective. Difficult problems are often difficult to overcome because you're too close to them—both physically and mentally. Travel at least once a year, and preferably take several trips throughout the year (a short weekend trip can be valuable).

7. Meditation can reduce your stress, calm your mind, and help you manage your thoughts. If possible, engage in a meditative practice every day.

Epilogue

The journey to become a self-disciplined producer never ends as there will always be specific areas to improve on. As with any journey, there will be ups and downs, temptations, frustrations, and failures. The modern world wants to capture your attention at any cost, and it will take constant vigilance on your part to say no and stay concentrated on what matters most to you.

Consequently, remember that to produce long-term results, you need to cultivate a consistent, committed routine of productivity-friendly habits and practices. Start small with one habit, and build on top of it, paying attention to do it all in a sustainable way that will help you stay productive for years and decades to come.

As a quick reminder of what we covered in this book, remember that:

1. A lack of attention will destroy your productivity. Practice your ability to concentrate by making sure that you limit your focus to the most

important task—and resist the temptation to leave it half-finished when you find yourself attracted to something else.

2. Embrace delayed gratification. As alluring as it is to believe that you can achieve your dreams in a matter of days or weeks, most goals take years, if not decades. Start working on your patience today.

3. Keeping things simple and working consciously—on the tasks you identified to be the most essential—is key to multiplying your productivity without working more (you can actually work less and still be more productive).

4. Exploring your limits will help you discover how much you can achieve in the short-term when you push yourself. You will also discover that your productivity is largely dependent on what you believe you're capable of accomplishing.

As important as being productive is, please don't forget that life isn't about work alone, though.

Work can give your life meaning, provide for your family, make the world a better place, and do a number of different things. However, none of this matters if your health doesn't let you enjoy the fruits of your labor or if your work obligations sever your ties with family and friends.

Bear this in mind and consider productivity-maximizing techniques a means to an end—a happier life *with* strong health and fulfilling relationships, not merely increased productivity while the rest of your life is in shambles.

I hope that by reading this book you've discovered some new strategies to help you become more productive and disciplined at work. My goal will be accomplished if you implement at least some suggestions from the book, so please help yourself by turning theory into real-world actions.

Download Another Book for Free

I want to thank you for buying my book and offer you another book (just as valuable as this one): *Grit: How to Keep Going When You Want to Give Up*, completely free.

Visit the link below to receive it:

http://www.profoundselfimprovement.com/sdp

In *Grit*, I'll tell you exactly how to stick to your goals, using proven methods from peak performers and science.

In addition to getting *Grit*, you'll also have an opportunity to get my new books for free, enter giveaways, and receive other valuable emails from me.

Again, here's the link to sign up:

http://www.profoundselfimprovement.com/sdp

Could You Help?

I'd love to hear your opinion about my book. In the world of book publishing, there are few things more valuable than honest reviews from a wide variety of readers.

Your review will help other readers find out whether my book is for them. It will also help me reach more readers by increasing the visibility of my book.

About Martin Meadows

Martin Meadows is the pen name of an author who has dedicated his life to personal growth. He constantly reinvents himself by making drastic changes in his life.

Over the years, he has regularly fasted for over 40 hours, taught himself two foreign languages, lost over 30 pounds in 12 weeks, run several businesses in various industries, took ice-cold showers and baths, lived on a small tropical island in a foreign country for several months, and wrote a 400-page novel's worth of short stories in one month.

But self-torture is not his passion. Martin likes to test his boundaries to discover how far his comfort zone goes.

His findings (based both on his personal experience and on scientific studies) help him improve his life. If you're interested in pushing your limits and learning how to become the best version of yourself, you'll love Martin's works.

You can read his books here:

http://www.amazon.com/author/martinmeadows.

[1] Haile, T. (2014, March 9). What You Think You Know About the Web Is Wrong. Retrieved August 24, 2017 from http://time.com/12933/what-you-think-you-know-about-the-web-is-wrong/.

[2] Ruedlinger, B. (2012, May 7). Does Video Length Matter? Retrieved August 24, 2017 from https://wistia.com/blog/does-length-matter-it-does-for-video-2k12-edition.

[3] Hiney, T., & MacShane, F. (Eds.) (2002). *The Raymond Chandler Papers: Selected Letters and Nonfiction 1909-1959*. Grove Press.

[4] http://www.pomodorotechnique.com/

[5] Tynan, (2012, October 22). If Not This One. Retrieved August 26, 2017 from http://tynan.com/thisone.

[6] Brooks, F. (1995). *The Mythical Man-Month: Essays on Software Engineering. Anniversary Edition*.

[7] Kois, D. (2012, March 29). Peter Dinklage Was Smart to Say No. Retrieved August 30, 2017 from http://www.nytimes.com/2012/04/01/magazine/peter-dinklage-was-smart-to-say-no.html.

[8] Epictetus (c. 108 A.D.). *Discourses of Epictetus*. Translated by Thomas Wentworth Higginson.

[9] Dickens, L., & DeSteno, D. (2016). The grateful are patient: Heightened daily gratitude is associated with attenuated temporal discounting. *Emotion*, 16(4): 421-425. doi: 10.1037/emo0000176.

[10] http://databank.worldbank.org/data/download/GDP_PPP.pdf

[11] Koch, R. (2011). *The 80/20 Principle: The Secret of Achieving More with Less*. Nicholas Brealey Publishing; 2 edition.

[12] Nielsen, J. (2006, October 9). The 90-9-1 Rule for Participation Inequality in Social Media and Online Communities. Retrieved September 1, 2017 from https://www.nngroup.com/articles/participation-inequality/.

[13] Keller, G., & Papasan, J. (2013). *The ONE Thing: The Surprisingly Simple Truth Behind Extraordinary Results*. John Murray.

[14] De Saint-Exupéry, A. (1939). *Wind, Sand and Stars*. Trans. Lewis Galantiere.

[15] My Name Is Danny Kavadlo. I Train Calisthenics. Retrieved September 4, 2017 from https://www.youtube.com/watch?v=La8YsLIfrPY.

[16] Parkinson, C. N. (1955, November 19). Parkinson's Law. Retrieved September 1, 2017 from http://www.economist.com/node/14116121.

[17] Hammond, C. (2016, September 27). How being alone may be the key to rest. Retrieved September 7, 2017 from http://www.bbc.com/news/magazine-37444982.

[18] Tyrväinen, L., Ojala, A., Korpela, K., Lanki, T., Tsunetsugu, Y., & Kagawa, T. (2014). The influence of urban green environments on stress relief measures: A field experiment. *Journal of Environmental Psychology*, 38: 1–9. doi: 10.1016/j.jenvp.2013.12.005.

[19] Bratman, G. N., Hamilton, J. P., Hahn, K. S., Daily, G. C., & Gross, J. J. (2015). Nature experience reduces rumination and subgenual prefrontal cortex activation. *Proceedings of the National Academy of Sciences*, 112(28): 8567–72. doi: 10.1073/pnas.1510459112.

[20] Bratman, G. N., Daily, G. C.; Levy, B. J., & Gross, J. J. (2015). The benefits of nature experience: Improved affect and cognition. *Landscape and Urban Planning*, 138: 41–50. doi:10.1016/j.landurbplan.2015.02.005.

[21] Baddeley, A. D. (1986). *Working memory*. Oxford University Press.

[22] University of Exeter (2013, July 9). Office plants boost well-being at work. Retrieved September 10, 2017 from http://www.exeter.ac.uk/news/research/title_306119_en.html.

[23] Cox, E. P., O'Dwyer, N., Cook, R., Vetter, M., Cheng, H. L., Rooney, K., & O'Connor, H. (2016). Relationship between physical activity and cognitive function in apparently healthy young to middle-aged adults: A systematic review. *Journal of Science and Medicine in Sport*. 19(8): 616–628. doi: 10.1016/j.jsams.2015.09.003.

[24] McMains, S., & Kastner, S. (2011). Interactions of top-down and bottom-up mechanisms in human visual cortex. *The Journal of Neuroscience*, 31(2): 587–597. doi: 10.1523/JNEUROSCI.3766-10.2011.

[25] Chiesa, A., & Serretti, A. (2009). Mindfulness-based stress reduction for stress management in healthy people: a review and meta-analysis. *Journal of Alternative and Complementary Medicine*, 15(5): 593–600. doi: 10.1089/acm.2008.0495.

79162077R00063

Made in the USA
San Bernardino, CA
12 June 2018